I0789154

5
Fundamental Reasons

Puerto Rico Can't Ever Be a State

by

Pepe Orraca

5 Fundamental Reasons

Copyright ©2017 Pepe Orraca
 José (Pepe) Orraca-Brandenberger
Calle San Sebastián, San Juan, Puerto Rico
pepeorraca@aol.com

If you would like to use material from this
book (other than for review purposes)
please contact the author / editor

"If admitted, Puerto Rico would be our most impoverished, least educated and most violent state."

Houston Young Republicans
January 24, 2017

Introduction

Political parties in Puerto Rico and their leadership have replaced good governance with the pursuit of status. All of them! By relying on its partisan ideology, it reduces the party's role in society to that of winning elections with the consequent abandonment of the responsibility to advance the living conditions of those who live on the island. The result has been a huge debt, long adopted and stimulated by both main parties. The spectacle of a free and associated state has vanished, while the actuality of the statehood proposal only gets as far as advertising slogans. Plus independence is a bad word.

Proponents of statehood for Puerto Rico loudly cry out that statehood is just about another plebiscite. This last one was the fifth. But the discourse does not inform that a federated statehood is not won by popular vote. And for the federal congress, those votes only represent the interest we ourselves may have in being annexed; not theirs.

It's the equivalent of sending them a box of chocolates with a note that reads: I like you a lot! An interest they may or may not reciprocate. It's important though to make clear that this political proposal to win statehood by votes is basically a deception that pretends to distract from bad government. The inclusion of Puerto Rico as a state does not depend on us. It totally depends on congress. That is why we will never be accepted as a state, no matter how we vote. The reasons are as simple as they are fundamental.

"...the union is a federation of similar sovereignties, different enough in their local interest to necessitate separate state government but so similar in common culture, language, and law as to make practical their binding as coequal participants under a federal government."

Houston Young Republicans
January 24, 2017

1st

Fundamental Reason

Historically, the process of converting territories into union states begins with territorial encroachment and the systematic invasion of American settlers; just as Israel is doing in the Palestinian territories. Once the immigrant population becomes numerically significant, they seize power structures and create their own governments, obviating the existence and needs of the original natives.

When that population reaches an absolute majority over the natives, which is achieved with the continuous invitation of new settlers, the population census' and lobbying of the federal legislature begins. A conversation between Americans; people who already understand each other and in the long run, when they have something to contribute to the union, they accept themselves as the brothers they are. To summarize, no Hawaiian native or Eskimo, devised seeking statehood for their nations.

The history of our Island is different. The Americans that come to the Island are here for a reason, whatever: employment, studies or marriage and after some time return to home. While they are here they stay among themselves, without venturing out too much to share with the natives. The few that do remain go 'Creole' and seek a niche that allows them to integrate into the Creole, local, society. They do not try to show off, nor seek to acquire positions in the power structures or become too visible in politics. However, the Americans who occupied Hawaii soon dethroned the legitimate Queen of these islands, banned the native religion, the use of native language,

and established their own government.

The US acquired Puerto Rico,
not because they needed to expand
their territory - as was the case with
Hawaii, to reach half across the Pa-
cific Ocean - but because they
wanted to prevent another European country from having a 'pied à
terre' in their America. They were
interested in the island of Puerto
Rico because of its strategic geo-
graphical location. Not to make it
part of the union. Just use it. The US
government was not interested in
flooding the island with American
immigrants, nor was it interested in

becoming a vocal part of local politics. The US was interested in building military bases and the infrastructure - electric power, roads, etc. - necessary to sustain the military apparatus that was being destined to the Island. Some people argue that granting us American citizenship proves the intent that we were to be part of the United States. The reality is that this 'half-breed' citizenship was another military addition. If we, Puerto Ricans, are all American citizens it then follows that any revolutionary, pro-independence, gesture could be considered treasonous to the homeland with the corresponding consequences. It was a creative way of saddling this new property with a collar and chain to keep it from running away.

After a hundred years lobbying for statehood we must recognize that Congress has no interest in it. All of congress' gestures in our favor have been political ploys to justify its continued possession of Puerto Rico, such as redefining Colony as a Commonwealth. The English translation of the contradictory Commonwealth reveals the issue.

According to Google Translate, *Estado Libre Asociado* in English is

Commonwealth, not a *Free Associate State*. In another dictionary Commonwealth only means an entity or political group; except when referring to Puerto Rico, then the translation is *Estado Libre Asociado*; a show of linguistic / political juggling which may be recognition of our political existence but shows zero commitment to Puerto Rico joining the union. Not even as an incorporated territory, a status precursor to becoming a state.

"...no territory deserves statehood by merit of anything other
than the national interest of the
United States'"

2nd

Fundamental Reason

The economy is the second reason why Puerto Rico is not going to become a state. The USA is a free enterprise capitalist country that idolizes money. Supports the entrepreneur, motivates productivity and embraces the acquisition of goods. The economic consequence of this attitude towards money is contempt for the poor and marginalized. It's with reluctance that US congresses approve palliative social programs that do not really solve anything, only postpone. Institutions of power insist that the poor are poor because they want to be poor. Because they're lazy! That's why they don't feel obliged to help the marginalized poor, nor to give them money. Money that the richest earned with the 'sweat of their brow'!

What's this got to do with it? Well, that Puerto Rico is a country of poor people. Of course, politicians confuse the issue by making comparisons with other Latin American and Caribbean countries. But they don't dare make comparison with a state where families of four,

22

with incomes of $ 40 thousand a year, are considered poor. In our Island a family with that kind of income can send their kids to private school. The average income in Puerto Rico is less than half the average income of the poorest state and by federal law more than half of our population, over 1.5 million, would be entitled to receive some form of federal assistance.

What kind of government, any government, far or near, could be interested in adding almost two million poor people to their entitlement programs? When, in addition, those two million poor people carry with them a devastated economy and negative population growth, which shrinks the state's tax base; the continued immigration to mainland USA of middle and professional class Puerto Ricans, means that everyday there will be less and less people on the island/state able to pay federal income tax.

Taking Puerto Rico in, either as a new arrondissement of Paris, incorporating us as a province of Spain or the granting of federated statehood would be political and financial craziness for the nation that picks us up. The economic potential that the Island promised has already been squandered by the continuous reverses in economic strategies and the excessive nature of our politicians struggling to win votes. We have nothing left to offer in favor of a federated statehood.

We are and will continue to be our own impediment to statehood.

"...that the interests of a distant island polity and those of a vast continental nation can never be so reconciled as to make just or practicable a union of government.

3rd
Fundamental Reason

Culture is the bitterest pill. We are a vibrant and active culture. And we are many. Our culture is so deeply rooted that only the extermination of the population could get it left behind. Forty years of public education only in English proves this. What purported to be a generational transformation of Puerto Ricans into Americans simply collapsed because of the absurdity of having Spanish speaking locals teaching in a language foreign to them, their students and the society they lived in. That's why it makes no sense to believe that a racist and nationalist nation wants to incorporate Puerto Rico intact, as equals, with our culture, sports identity, legal system and a language that is foreign to Americans. The US government was able to push the Eskimos into a corner to make it easy to take control over that vast territory they had bought. In Puerto Rico there is no corner where to push us.

The anxiety of those politicians that want to stuff statehood down our throats is out of fear. They fear that the USA will abandon

us. Those strategic and military ad-
vantages we offered have faded.
Our economy is bankrupt; commer-
cially exploitable natural resources
are non-existent and the immense
debt that the government has in-
curred makes Puerto Rico a net loss.
We are like a boyfriend who got old,
fat and ugly, looking for a quick
marriage before they get a 'Dear
John' letter. That's what's behind
the urgency.

The cost of raising living
standards in Puerto Rico to any kind
of comparable with the other 50
states would be unreasonable for
the other states, since we have

nothing to contribute. A large part of the US population rejects bilingual education and / or any accommodation for the Spanish-speaking population. The idea of a special Puerto Rican state, "*Estadidad Jíbara*" as has been proposed, is a constitutional impossibility.

Is there a politician, here or there, who honestly believes that the integration of our nation with theirs is a great idea for America? Is there a politician, here or there, who honestly thinks statehood for us would be for the benefit of the USA?

32

So, what's the deal? It's simpler than it seems. Education in a colony comes with some degradation attached. In our case it was: 'Puerto Rico is a very small, poor island, without any kind of resources, incapable of sustaining itself'. This has led many to be ashamed of being Puerto Rican. By embracing an alien culture/nation, the rejection of their-own nationality/culture is implicit. It's not that the pro-statehood constituency want to be American, what they don't want to be is Puerto Rican. Therefore the need for deception!

If the passion for statehood were honest, they would have gone to live in the United States, as many have. But their preference is to destroy what is central to being Puerto Rican. As if it was an offering to the deity America. Thinking that in sacrificing our nation, our children's heritage, we will achieve the acceptance of the usurpers of our land.

And that is known as the Stockholm Syndrome!

"...separated by geography, language, law, culture, and governing custom, the people of Puerto Rico constitute a body politic unto themselves; that theirs is a political culture separate and distinct from that of the states of our federal union."

Houston Young Republicans
January 24, 2017

4th

Fundamental Reason

Puerto Rico would be the first colonial territory seeking to become a federal state, which already has a national entity (polity) of its own and I don't just mean culture. When the USA bought the island, Puerto Rico was organized politically, legally and religiously. What only really changed in 1898 was who appointed the new governor, because we even had a palace where to put him; but, of course, everything in Spanish with a European flair. The 19th century Conquerors preferred to leave most things as they were and simply add or improve as they saw the need. They did not have to fix what wasn't broken.

As a colony we were a bargain. As a state we are a problem. Obvious differences, such as language and appearance, are monumental in themselves, but there are so many other major and minor differences that the unification of Puerto Rico to the nation would have to be a process of reconstruction. Like the political process of the forced reintegration of the confederate states after the civil war: to get rid of what exists, the old, so as to build the 'new'. But then, the legitimate question is: Who is going to carry out the task?

You have to be hallucinating if you believe that the same local politicians who put us in the $72 billion hole we're in, have the capability to carry out that reconstruction. What has not happen during the more than 100 years of colonialism, the American political parties with their multimillion-dollar political machines are going to dock on the island and run their own stateside political hacks as Puerto Rico's candidates for federal legislative posi-

tions. They - the new 'carpet bag-
gers' - are going to claim superiori-
ty over us natives in knowledge and
experience about federal matters.
And rightly so, for many! But then
right behind those first intruders
we'll see the real hustlers arrive.
We'll be fresh meat for political vul-
tures.

I'm not exaggerating. It's the
political version of the megastores'
history on the island. Local businesses, small, disappear against the
brutal competition of millionaire
budgets and their national supply
web. To visualize what I'm saying,
simply replace the Democratic Party

with Sam's Club and the Republican Party with Costco. Local parties (businesses) are assimilated and disappear. Local affairs will continue to be handled by the natives (store managers) in Spanish, but all matters of consequence will be handled by the American regional chiefs in English. Same as, let's say, Walgreen's today.

Let's take a good look at this: the Americanization of the local constitution, the Americanization of the Codes of Law, Civil and Criminal, the reconstruction of tax systems with a federal income tax at its center, plus the re-building of a minimized state government, are just some of the necessary governmental / social upheavals that will happen.

The big question, for me, is where are we, the native Puerto Ricans going to be after that apocalypse? Like the Hawaiians? A sort of consortium of employees owned by American corporations and politicians? If we don't really own our land now, what about in that future that no one wants to tell us much about? Will we be major stockholders or merely sharecroppers on the estate property of some off-island tycoon?

"...political corruption in Puerto Rico is endemic and structural, embedded in its political economy and unlikely to be corrected..."

Houston Young Republicans
January 24, 2017

5th

Fundamental Reason

When considering a new part-
ner or a new state for the union you
don't only focus on financial matters and the number of votes in favor, the character of the applicant is
also evaluated. It is called moral sol-
vency. I remember once reading
with amazement the local paper's
headline that the head of the Mafia
on the island was a police colonel
(Alejo Maldonado). Government

employees responsible for burning previously used food stamps thought they were better recycled. They arrested about twelve.

The feds shut down the passport office on the Island because the employees in charge sold them unceremoniously. On this island not only drivers' licenses and birth certificates were sold outright. Virtually every official document was available for sale at some point. Even the license to practice medicine could be bought! FBI surveillance has brought down lawmakers, mayors and government agency clerks and sent to jail. They have published corruption schemes at all levels of government, banking and finance with their subsequent arrests.

Corruption in Puerto Rico's local government is institutionalized. Political corruption goes beyond the immoral. Corruption here is a mind frame. Everything is looked at through the spy-glass of status, not the reality that we live. If a proposal is linked to the political strategy of the party, read status, the proposal is given a green light; no matter what it really costs, no matter how much is stolen from it.

The proponents of the statehood referendum want us to believe that with a majority of votes now, we will somehow pull off the goal of permanent union, afterwards, as if the daily reality of fraud against Medicare, fraud with federal programs, bank fraud, constant violations of environmental regulations, federal court order violations, civil liberties, etc. The most effective argument for putting a hold on possible statehood is the widespread corruption in our government and its institutions.

Some will argue that it's not as bad as it seems that the media exaggerate the scope of corruption. It's true that Puerto Rico is stuck only between Greece and Dominica on the list of bad guys. It's also true that in that list of corrupt countries there are more than 90 countries 'worse' than us. But if we make the comparison with the states in the nation that we wish to join, we would be the most corrupt state of that nation. We would be at the very bottom of the barrel.

As the saying goes: One rotten apple spoils the whole barrel!

Wrap Up
5 Fundamental Reasons

These essays are not a condemnation of the ideal of statehood. It is a direct criticism of the politicians who with deceit take advantage of the genuine aspirations of the people. It is a critique of those politicians who promoted and have obtained gain from the economic debacle; and who now want to distract us, with flags and status celebrations, from the all-important hunt for the missing $ 72 billion Puerto Rico now owes.

Ever since someone wrote the jingle 'this has got to change' in 1968, a lyrical federated status named 'jíbaro statehood' has been promoted: a state where we get everything our way without paying anything for it. They also lie to people when they say that our representation in international events will continue despite statehood. As if it was an acquired right. They lie again when they say that our identity as a nation is going to be preserved. These are lies designed to confuse those who do not know the history, the constitution, nor the laws of the United States.

If that were true, then how come neither New York nor California have Olympic teams? The US constitution has made it clear in all instances that no state of the union can have privileges, benefits or disadvantages over other states. Why the lie? Because if they tell the truth, they would have to admit that you cannot be both American and Puerto Rican at the same time.

Our politicians do everything in theory. In the abstract! They build castles or trains in the air that are unsustainable when the foundations have to be reality. They promote entrepreneurship as a solution to unemployment without considering that all these new businesses need a clientele with money to spend. They pass laws that no one respects but capture votes, announce statistics that suit them and promise villas without having the money to pay them.

All the proposals on statehood thrown at us only reach the first base. None gets to 'home'. No one has ever explained to us what comes later; after becoming a state. In reality, the statehood proposal is all about advertising slogans, as if economic well-being and good governance are magically infused with statehood.

Puerto Rico has a colonial history peppered with illegalities, colored with native buccaneers, noble pirates, corrupt governors and the consistent misuse of public funds for over 500 years. Right now, it should surprise that we have a stable underground economy of the same size and significance as the 'legal' economy of the now bankrupt government. Drug dealing has not lost a foothold and politicians continue to gain weight.

After statehood there is no turning back. Even after becoming a full-fledged republic we can still change our mind, like Texas did. Of all the status options, statehood is the only permanent, eternal proviso. With statehood we lose the right to change our minds. That's why all Americans and Puerto Ricans have to look carefully at what statehood is really all about. We don't want to trade for the same or worse.

Without being critical of that great nation of the United States of America, we must ask ourselves why the Puerto Rican who lives in the US is much more nationalistic than the Puerto Rican who lives here on the Island. How come?

Afterword

This letter I'm including is not an official Republican Party document nor does it represent the Republican Party's position on the acceptance of Puerto Rico as a state of the union. As it reads it's the unanimous motion of the Houston Young Republicans presented on the floor of the **Texas Young Republican Federation's** quarterly board meeting. Although it may not be backed by officialdom, it does sum up all the objections that Republicans or Democrats could argue against Puerto Rico becoming a state. What's important is that until now, no political organization in the USA has formally expressed in writing what Puerto Ricans living in the US experience every day. That's how numerous groups of Americans see us, Puerto Ricans and this is how they'll talk about us.

Original Text in English

"On January 24th, 2017, the Houston Young Republicans voted with no objections for the following resolution to be submitted to the Texas Young Republican Federation's quarterly board meeting:

Whereas the Resident Commissioner of Puerto Rico has introduced a bill to the House of Representatives seeking to have Puerto Rico admitted as a state to our federal union.

Whereas a resolution has been submitted for the consideration of the Young Republican National Federation's quarterly meeting that supports the prospect of statehood for Puerto Rico.

Whereas it is the founding principle of this nation that the interests of a distant island polity and those of a vast continental nation can never be so reconciled as to make just or practicable a union of government.

Whereas it is in the best interests of justice, efficiency of administration, and the preservation of popular sovereignty, that separate and distinct political cultures operate according to their own custom and under their own sovereignties.

Whereas that the founding assumption of our constitution is that the union is a federation of similar sovereignties, different enough in their local interest to necessitate separate state government but so similar in common culture, language, and law as to make practical their binding as coequal participants under a federal government.

Whereas that being so separated by geography, language, law, culture, and governing custom, the people of Puerto Rico constitute a body politic unto themselves; that theirs is a political culture separate and distinct from that of the states of our federal union.

Whereas our founding beliefs hold that injustice would result in allowing what is in fact a foreign political culture to potentially bind those in a system that does not share its particular assumptions and worldviews, and simultaneously an injustice would result in allowing our own culture to come to dominate and replace the traditions of another.

Whereas making Puerto Rico a state – the full annexation and integration of a colonial possession with a separate political identity- would render us an empire in the political science sense of the word.

Whereas as Republicans we are also republicans: we wish to maintain the good sense republican position against overseas imperial pretense.

Whereas potential admission of a territory as a state must be viewed upon its own merits – no territory deserves statehood by merit of anything other than the national interest of the United States. It is for this reason that the push to make the territorial Philippines a state failed, as did Mormon superstate Deseret and explicitly Native American Sequoyah.

Whereas Puerto Rico has limited natural resources, little modern strategic significance, less average education, and very high rates of poverty, unemployment, crime, and corruption. If admitted, Puerto Rico would be our most impoverished, least educated and most violent state.

Whereas the political corruption in Puerto Rico is endemic and structural, embedded in its political economy and unlikely to be corrected simply by arresting notable participants.

Whereas allowing such corruption to exist in a coequal state in our federal system would be a national embarrassment. Any meaningful attempt to fix this, however, would be perceived by those on the island as an imposition. If the history of big city corruption prosecutions is any guide, attempts to clean the government of the island would be painted by Democrats as a racist attempt to lock up the genuine voices of underprivileged and underserved communities.

Whereas the government of the island reflects the traditional Latin American political reality of a wealthy Castellano elite ruling over a mixed race population, with status in the civil service correlating to placement along the pardo/white axis. The admission of a state based upon these lines cannot improve race relations.

Whereas traditionally conservative and Republican political positions remain unpopular on the island, while support for far reaching government regulation, gun control, an expansive civil service, and an extensive welfare system are very popular.

Whereas the political history of the island makes it clear that their admission as a state would provide two new reliably Democratic Senate seats, reliable Democratic votes in the Electoral College, and a majori-ty-Democratic House delegation.

Whereas making Puerto Rico a state would provide ammunition for the push to make the District of Co-lumbia a state, as the Left uses any victory as a pretext for their next similar leap.

Whereas admission of Puerto Rico as a state would necessitate that America become officially bi-lingual and that this would increase the normalization of non-use of English with an inevitable decline in our cultural desire and ability to as-similate immigrants, especially Spanish speaking ones.

Whereas making Puerto Rico a state would subject it to the full brunt of federal regulation and un-funded mandates, further bogging

down its long term economic pro-
spects.

Whereas the ruction and intra-
party strife from this past electoral
cycle has shown us the dangers of a
party hierarchy seen to align with
the left on important national identity issues.

Whereas we believe the economic and political issues that face
Puerto Rico can be addressed fairly
and adequately without the radical
solution of granting them statehood.

Whereas Puerto Rico's Spanish language civil law legal system already presents hurdles when enforcing full faith and credit and for mainland courts sitting in diversity jurisdiction. Should statehood increase the problems these issues present to judicial economy, the administration of justice would suffer as a result.

Therefore be it resolved that the Texas Young Republican Federation opposes the admission of Puerto Rico as a state, encourages the elected representatives of the people of Texas to oppose the same, and encourages the Young

Republican National Federation to reject any resolution in its favor."

Translation to Spanish

"El 24 de enero de 2017, los Jóvenes Republicanos de Houston votaron sin objeciones para que la siguiente resolución fuera presentada a la reunión trimestral de la Federación Republicana de Jóvenes de Texas:

Considerando que el Comisionado Residente de Puerto Rico ha presentado un proyecto de ley a la Cámara de Representantes que busca que Puerto Rico sea admitido como estado a nuestra unión federal.

Considerando que se ha presentado una resolución para la consideración de la reunión trimestral de la Federación Nacional de Jóvenes Republicanos que respalda la perspectiva de un estado para Puerto Rico.

Mientras que es el principio fundador de esta nación que los intereses políticos de una isla lejana y los de una vasta nación continental nunca pueden llegar a ser tan reconciliados como para hacer justo o práctico una unión de gobierno.

Considerando que es en el mejor interés de la justicia, la

eficiencia de la administración y la preservación de la soberanía popular, que culturas políticas, separadas y distintas, operen según sus propias costumbres y bajo sus propias soberanías.

Considerando que la suposición fundamental de nuestra constitución es que la unión es una federación de soberanías similares, suficientemente diferentes en sus intereses locales como para exigir un gobierno estatal distinto, pero similar en cultura, lenguaje y leyes como para hacer práctico su vinculación como participantes iguales bajo un gobierno federal.

Considerando que siendo separados por la geografía, el idioma, el derecho legal, la cultura y la gobernanza, el pueblo de Puerto Rico constituye de por sí, un cuerpo político propio. Siendo que la suya es una cultura política separada y distinta de la de los estados de nuestra unión federal.

Mientras que nuestras creencias fundamentales mantienen que el resultaría en una injusticia permitir que una cultura política foránea, que de hecho es, se ligue potencialmente a un sistema que no comparte su particular visión del mundo ni sus preconcepciones. Y simultáneamente resultaría en una injusticia permitir que nuestra propia cultura llegue a dominar y reemplazar las tradiciones del otro.

Considerando que hacer de Puerto Rico un estado -la anexión completa e integración de una posesión colonial con una identidad política separada- nos convertiría en un Imperio en el sentido de la ciencia política.

Que mientras Republicanos somos también republicanos: deseamos mantener la sensata posición republicana contra la pretensión imperial de ultramar.

Mientras que la admisión potencial de un territorio como estado debe considerarse por sus propios méritos - ningún territorio merece la condición de Estado por méritos que no sean del interés nacional de los Estados Unidos. Es por esta razón que el empuje para hacer el Filipinas territorial un estado fracasó, al igual que el superestado mormón Deseret y la gestión claramente nativo americano de Sequoyah.

Considerando que Puerto Rico tiene limitados recursos naturales, poca importancia estratégica moderna, menos educación promedio y tasas muy altas de pobreza, desempleo, crimen y corrupción. Si se admite, Puerto Rico sería nuestro estado más empobrecido, menos educado y más violento.

Mientras que la corrupción política en Puerto Rico es endémica y estructural, incrustada en su economía política y poco probable que se corrija simplemente arrestando los participantes más reconocibles.

Mientras que permitir que tal corrupción exista en nuestro sistema federal como un igual sería una vergüenza nacional. Cualquier intento significativo de arreglar esto, sin embargo, sería percibido por los de la Isla como una imposición. Si la historia de los enjuiciamientos por corrupción en las grandes ciudades es una guía, los intentos de limpiar el gobierno de la isla serán pintados por los demócratas como un intento racista de bloquear las voces genuinas de las comunidades desfavorecidas y desatendidas.

Mientras que el gobierno de la isla refleja la realidad política tradicional latinoamericana de una casta (Castallano) rica y elite gobernando sobre una población de raza mixta, con una situación que se correlaciona con la colocación a lo largo del eje pardo / blanco. La admisión de un estado basado en estas líneas no va a poder mejorar las relaciones raciales.

Mientras que las posiciones políticas tradicionalmente conservadoras y republicanas siguen siendo poco populares en la isla, mientras que el apoyo a la regulación gubernamental de largo alcance, el control de armas, un servicio civil expansivo, y un sistema de bienestar extenso son muy populares.

Mientras que la historia política de la isla deja claro que su admisión como estado proporcionaría dos nuevos asientos confiablemente demócratas en el Senado, votos confiablemente demócratas en el

Colegio Electoral y una delegación mayoritariamente demócrata para la legislatura.

Considerando que hacer de Puerto Rico un estado proporcionaría municiones para el esfuerzo de hacer del Distrito de Columbia un estado, ya que la izquierda usa cualquier victoria como pretexto para su próximo salto similar.

Mientras que la admisión de Puerto Rico como estado requeriría que Estados Unidos se volviera oficialmente bilingüe; y que esto aumentaría la normalización del no-uso del inglés con una inevitable disminución de nuestra capacidad y deseo cultural de asimilar inmigrantes, especialmente los hispanohablantes.

Considerando que hacer que Puerto Rico fuera un estado lo sometería a todo el peso de la regulación federal y de los mandatos sin fondos, complicando aún más sus perspectivas económicas a largo plazo.

En la medida en que la discusión y las luchas intra-partidista de este último ciclo electoral nos han mostrado los peligros de que una jerarquía partidaria se vea alineada con la izquierda sobre importantes cuestiones de identidad nacional.

Considerando que las cuestiones económicas y políticas que encara Puerto Rico se puede abordar de manera justa y adecuada sin la solución radical de concederles la estadidad.

Considerando que el sistema jurídico de derecho civil de Puerto Rico ya presenta obstáculos para hacer cumplir con plena fe y crédito y para los tribunales continentales que se encuentran en la jurisdicción de diversidad. Si la estadidad aumenta los problemas en estas cuestiones de economía judicial, la administración de justicia sufriría como resultado.

Por lo tanto, se resuelve que la Federación Republicana de Jóvenes de Texas se opone a la admisión de Puerto Rico como estado, alienta a los representantes electos de la gente de Texas para oponerse a la misma, y alienta a la Federación Nacional Jóvenes Republicanos a rechazar cualquier resolución en su favor."

Author

Pepe Orraca is also author of the Spanish version of this book, *5 Razones y un Epílogo* (Amazon, Kindle);

La Histeria Económica de Puerto Rico (Casa Norberto, Amazon, Kindle) and regularly publishes his opinions in his blog:

La Terapia de Pepe Orraca (www.pepeorraca.blogspot.com)